GLADIATORS

Minna Lacey & Susanna Davidson

Illustrated by
Emmanuel Cerisier

History consultant: Dr. Verity Platt,
University of Oxford

Contents

*A note on dates: early dates are written as "**BC**", which stands for "**B**efore **C**hrist". BC dates are counted back from the year 1, the traditional date for the birth of Jesus Christ. The bigger a number, the longer ago the date.*

CHAPTER 1

Who were the gladiators?

Admired by men and adored by women, gladiators were trained fighters who entertained huge crowds in Ancient Rome. The most famous gladiators had large followings of loyal fans, just like football stars today.

Dressed to impress in shining metals, with rippling muscles on show, gladiators fought in arenas all over the Roman Empire. They entered to wild cheers from the crowd.

Most gladiators were slaves, criminals or prisoners of war, sold to gladiator owners and forced to fight. To keep spectators glued to their seats, they had to fight bravely, risking life and limb every time they fought. But not all fights were to the death. Gladiators were expensive to train and keep, so dead ones were a waste of money.

Successful gladiators could go on to win fight after fight and were richly rewarded with prize money and female fans. Some men even *chose* to become gladiators, either to win admiration or in the desperate hope of paying off debts.

Women also fought as gladiators, although much less often than men. One emperor, the insane Domitian, apparently liked to watch them fight dwarves by candlelight. But usually women fought against each other.

Some people found women gladiators disgusting. "See her neck bent down under the weight of her helmet," wrote the poet Juvenal, "...her legs look like tree trunks." Emperor Severus agreed, and in the year 200 he banned women from fighting altogether.

It would have been boring if gladiators all fought the same way. Over the years, many different fighting styles developed.

Retiarius (plural - retiarii)

Secutor (plural - secutores)

Retiarii used tridents to knock out opponents, then trapped them in their nets. The only gladiators to fight without a helmet or shield.

Secutores were usually paired against the *retiarii*. They had smooth helmets to avoid being caught by the nets.

Murmillo (plural - murmillones)

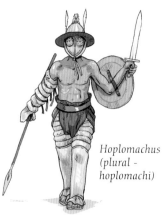

Hoplomachus (plural - hoplomachi)

Murmillones were known as fish men because they had an image of a fish carved on their helmets. Their only weapon was the sword.

Hoplomachi used their lances as their first weapon. If they lost their lances, they would use their daggers instead.

By the first century, these had become set, with particular weapons and techniques for each type of gladiator.

Thraex (plural - thraeces)

Samnite (plural - samnites)

Thraeces dressed like fighters from Thrace, in northern Greece. They used their curved swords to snake past heavier opponents' shields.

Samnites were heavily armed with large shields and short swords. They wore helmets with a visor and a crest.

Eques (plural - equites)

Provocator (plural - provocatores)

Equites entered the arena on horseback carrying lances, but finished on foot, fighting with swords.

Provocatores usually fought other men in their own category. The only gladiators to wear full breastplates.

Essedarius (plural - essedarii)

Essedarii stormed into the arena on war-chariots, driven at terrifying speeds, and finished fighting on foot with swords. They usually fought against each other.

Laquerarius (plural - laquerarii)

Dimachaerius (plural - dimachaeri)

Laquerarii were similar to the retiarii, but used lassos instead of nets to trap their opponents.

Dimachaeri fought with daggers and wore little protective clothing.

*Andabatus
(plural -
andabatae)*

*Sagittarius
(plural -
sagittari)*

Andabatae wore helmets without eye holes. They charged blindly at each other on horseback.

Sagittari were archers dressed in pointed helmets. Their long-range bows could shoot over 200m (655ft).

*Venator
(plural -
venatores)*

Venatores were trained hunters of wild animals. Not strictly gladiators, but an important part of the show. They were assisted by the *bestiarii* who had to look after the animals and provoked them during the fights.

CHAPTER II

The first games

The very first gladiator fights were held at the funeral celebrations of important Roman officials, with pairs of slaves fighting to the death as part of the festivities.

Some Romans thought the idea had come from the Etruscans, whose kings had been very powerful in the early days of Rome. The Etruscans killed prisoners at the funerals of brave warriors. They believed this would please the spirits of the dead warriors and help them reach the next world. The aim was to stop their ghosts from coming back to haunt the living.

But we now think the Romans got their idea for gladiator fights from the Greek people who had settled in Campania, in southern Italy.

The Greeks didn't just have human sacrifices
at funerals – they had funeral contests, with
chariot races, fist fights and fighting warriors.

The first recorded gladiator fight in Rome
took place in 264 BC. A man named Decimus
Junius Brutus arranged for three pairs of slaves
to fight to the death at his father's funeral.

"We'll have it in the main cattle market,"
Decimus decided. "So everyone can watch."

On the day of the funeral, a huge crowd gathered outside.

"Let the contest begin," announced the organizer.

The first pair of slaves stepped up to each other and lunged forward with a clash of steel. The crowd gasped. In a few minutes one slave had stabbed his opponent to death. The spectators clapped and shouted. Two more fights followed, until three slaves lay dead on the ground.

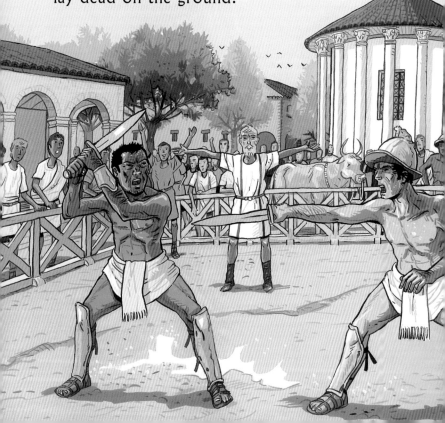

The spectacle was a great success. People talked about nothing else for weeks. Soon, every wealthy Roman was planning to have a contest at his funeral.

Romans hoped to outdo their rivals with more and more extravagant events. A hundred years later, a Roman general Titus Quinctius Flaminius had an incredible 74 gladiator fights at his funeral. It went on for three whole days.

Here you can see the protective clothing worn by most gladiators.

Helmet - generally made of thick, sheet bronze. Its average weight was about 4kg (9 lbs).

Manica - a thickly-padded linen or leather arm guard strapped on to the sword arm.

The upper body was usually left bare, as a sign of a gladiator's readiness to die.

Gladius - a gladiator's sword. Swords ranged from medium length weapons with broad, straight blades, to very short ones – more like daggers – with very sharp points.

Greaves - protective metal leg wear, held in place with leather straps, threaded through eyelets. Padding was worn underneath to stop the greaves from pressing down on the tops of the feet.

Shield - provided protection against the thrusting blows of an opponent. Often made from a kind of plywood and covered in leather. Gladiators with smaller shields wore longer greaves, and vice versa.

Over time, fighters began to wear protective clothing, to make the fights last longer. Each fighter carried a short sword called a *gladius*, which is how gladiators got their name.

Soon, gladiator fights were more about gaining power for the living than spilling blood to please the dead. At this time, Rome was ruled by an elected council called the Senate, made up of men called senators. Wealthy noblemen and generals wanting to become senators quickly realized that putting on gladiator shows was one of the best ways to win votes.

In 90 BC, a Roman general named Sulla organized a gladiator fight with prisoners of war from Samnium, in southeast Italy. The Samnites were a tribe of fierce warriors and the contest was spectacular. Sulla was soon elected Consul, the top job in the Senate.

By the time of Rome's first emperor, Augustus, gladiator fights had become one of the most popular forms of entertainment. Staging spectacular fights was now an essential way for rulers to hold onto power.

CHAPTER III

Gladiator school

S pecial gladiator training schools, called
ludi, were scattered all over the Roman
Empire. Their owners, the *lanistae*, were
usually old gladiators whose fighting days
were over. They made their money by
renting out gladiators or selling them
on for the best price.

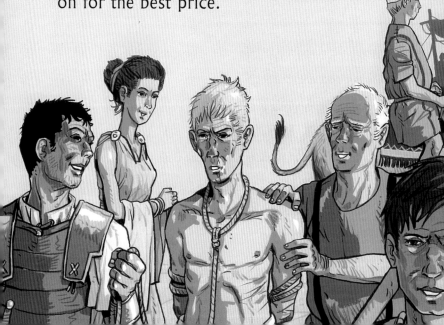

The *lanistae* spent their time touring slave markets, looking for men with the right build and fitness, then training them to be fighting machines.

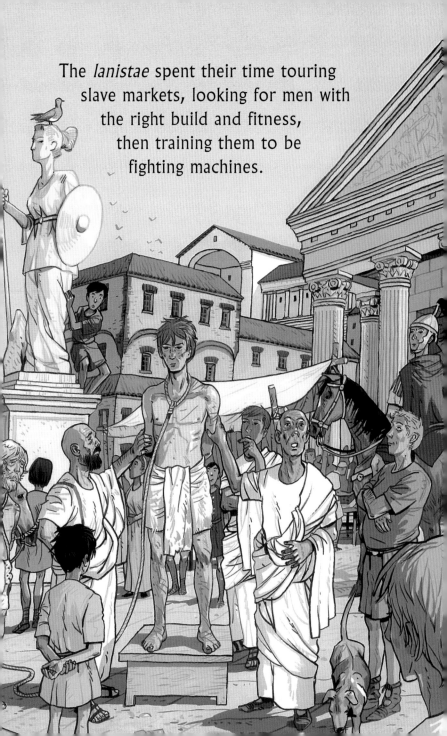

Starting gladiator school was terrifying. First, a student had to swear, "I accept the whip, the branding iron and the sword to punish me" – a reminder that he was a slave and would be punished if he did anything wrong.

For prisoners of war who couldn't speak Latin (the Roman language), it was easy to make mistakes. They often ended up in the school prison, which was a grim place to stay. The prison in Pompeii had heavy iron leg chains and low ceilings, so inmates could only sit down.

Gladiators slept in small, dark cells and were guarded at all times. But the *lanistae* had to take care of their gladiators to make sure they performed well. So they hired the best doctors, cooks and masseurs, and fed their men boiled beans, oatmeal and barley grains. Doctors thought this would help to stop them from bleeding to death. Gladiators were sometimes called *hordearii*, meaning "barley men", because of their diet.

Students trained with blunt weapons, swiping at a man of straw or a *palus* (a wooden post) to build up their muscles. The *lanistae* watched their new recruits closely to decide which style of fighting would suit them best.

The same group of gladiators trained together every day. But it was hard to know who to trust. A gladiator could be enjoying breakfast with an inmate in the morning – and have to fight him in the arena that afternoon.

The larger schools had training grounds with seats for spectators. Knowing how to please a crowd was the gladiator's best chance of survival. They all needed to learn to fight with flourish – and fast.

CHAPTER IV

The stadium

At first gladiator fights took place just about anywhere – market places, open spaces in towns, called *forums*, and even in fields. As the shows became more popular, special stadiums were built out of wood. But these turned out to be death traps for both spectators and gladiators. Many caught fire, or collapsed during shows. Then, in around 80 BC, the first stone stadiums were built. Soon, they were popping up all over Italy, and in every important Roman settlement abroad.

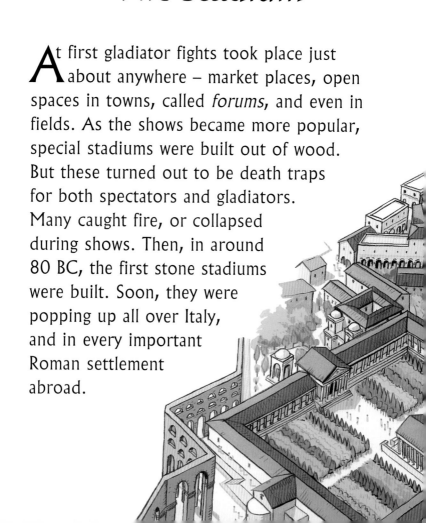

But there was one that surpassed all others in size, engineering and magnificence: the Colosseum in Rome.

The Colosseum was built right in the middle of the city. Nearby was the Ludus Magnus (in the bottom right of this picture), the most important gladiator school. An underground passage linked it directly to the arena in the Colosseum.

The Colosseum was started by Emperor Vespasian in the year 70. He hired the best architects and craftsmen to build the biggest stadium Rome had ever seen.

Ingeniously constructed to seat 50,000 spectators, it was even larger than most football stadiums today. The arena floor was oval-shaped, to give spectators close-up views of the action and to stop players from hiding in corners. The columns and seats were made entirely from white marble, and there was even a canvas awning to shade the audience on hot days.

The emperor had his own private entrance which led directly to his imperial box. There were two grand entrances for senators, priests and foreign leaders, while everyone else flocked in through 76 numbered archways.

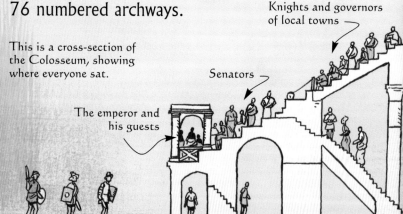

Knights and governors of local towns

This is a cross-section of the Colosseum, showing where everyone sat.

Senators

The emperor and his guests

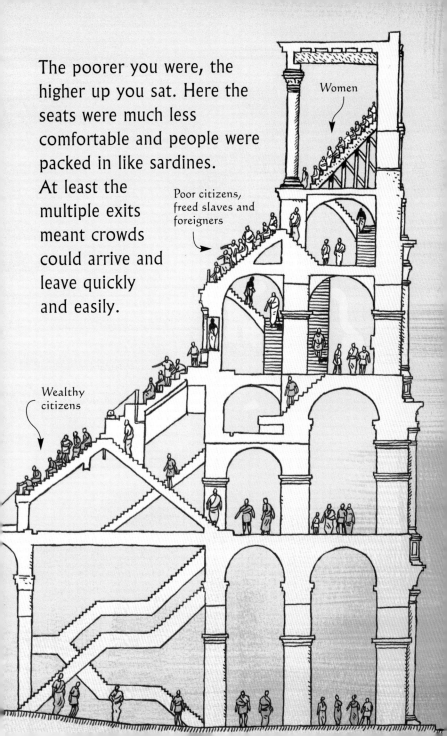

The poorer you were, the higher up you sat. Here the seats were much less comfortable and people were packed in like sardines. At least the multiple exits meant crowds could arrive and leave quickly and easily.

Women

Poor citizens, freed slaves and foreigners

Wealthy citizens

The Colosseum took ten years to build and the emperor died before it was finished. So it was his son, Titus, who opened the Colosseum with a lavish 100-day festival. This included gladiator fights and wild beast hunts, in which 9,000 animals were killed.

People from all over the Empire came to the opening event. "The Sarmatians come, their lips still wet with horses' blood," wrote the Roman poet Martial. "What race is so distant, so barbarous, Emperor, that no spectator from there is in your city?"

Several years later, the floor was rebuilt with a maze of underground rooms, where wild animals were kept in cages. A few hours before a performance, the gates on the cages were lifted. The animals were then forced down a narrow passageway and into lifts, which carried them up to the arena floor.

1 - Animals were loaded into the lifts. At a signal, slave teams hoisted the cages, via a pulley system, up to the arena floor.

2 - At a second signal, a rope was pulled to release a trap door in the arena floor.

Over time, the Colosseum became a symbol of Rome itself. A popular saying declared:
When the Colosseum falls, Rome will fall,
When Rome falls, the world will fall...
...but, while Rome fell 1,500 years ago, the Colosseum still stands, and remains one of the greatest masterpieces of world architecture.

3 - At the same time the cage was opened, freeing the animal, which leaped, terror-stricken, to face the spectators.

CHAPTER V

A day at the Colosseum

In the weeks leading up to a big gladiator event, posters start appearing on the walls in Rome. Professional graffiti artists advertise the show by carving messages wherever they can – on shop walls and even on gravestones.

Tickets are expensive, so people rush to get their hands on the free ones being given out by the emperor's servants.

On the night before the games, a huge feast is held for the gladiators. Some gorge themselves on the fine food, while others just stare into space, sick at the thought of tomorrow's slaughter.

By dawn, thousands of spectators have already taken their seats. Talking is difficult, as the sound of trumpeting elephants and roaring lions is deafening. The animals haven't been fed for days – to make them more eager to fight.

The crowd cheers as two tigers burst through the trap doors. At first they are too dazed to move, but they are quickly whipped into action. This will be a fight to the death.

Next up are the circus acts. A team of trained elephants performs a dance and a boy rides on the back of a bear. The crowd claps, but some people are impatient for the *venatio* – men and animals in head-on combat. Today it's the turn of Carpophorus, a well-known fighter, famous for taking on lions. By lunchtime, the arena is soaked in blood.

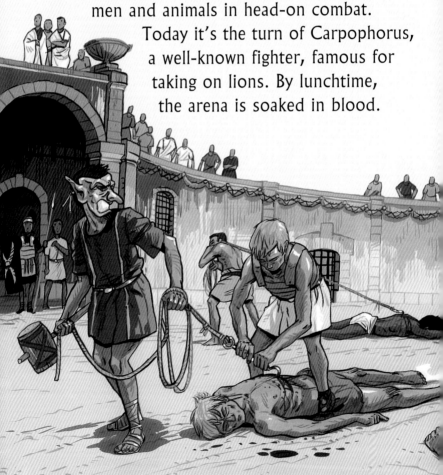

Some people get up to take a break from the violence. But most stay seated to watch the execution of condemned criminals. They enter the arena weaponless and are quickly mauled to death by yet more ravenous wild animals.

Then two eerie figures appear. Their task is to inspect the bodies. One is dressed as Hermes, the messenger of the gods; the other as Charon, ferryman to the underworld. Hermes prods the bodies with a red-hot iron to check that they're dead. Then Charon drags the corpses away.

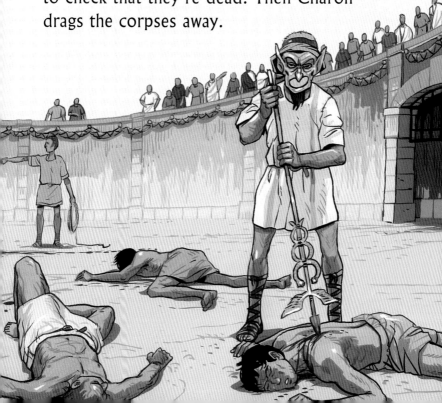

The crowd finally falls silent to watch the gladiator procession. As they parade around the arena, the emperor inspects their weapons, to make sure they are sharp enough to cause as much damage as possible.

Then, with a blast of trumpets and horns, the first gladiators begin to fight. It's a *retiarius*, a net-fighter, against a heavily-armed *secutor*. The *retiarius* moves nimbly around the arena, trying to hit the *secutor* with his trident. His opponent dodges out of the way.

The *secutor* advances slowly forward, clutching his sword. For forty minutes the two are locked in deadly combat, putting the tricks of their training into practice.

But the *retiarius* has the advantage of surprise. At the last minute he switches his trident to his left hand and strikes, catching the *secutor* off-guard. The next moment the *retiarius* has trapped the *secutor* under his lead-weighted net. Then he moves in for the face-off, his short dagger at the ready.

By this time the horns and trumpets are playing frenzied music, and the crowd is shouting, "*Habet, hoc habet!*" ("Got him, he's had it!") as loud as they can. The defeated *secutor* asks them for mercy by lifting the index finger of his left hand.

Some think the *secutor* has fought a good fight, and are shouting "*Mitte!*" ("Let him go!"), and waving their handkerchiefs. But most are turning their thumbs*, to show they think he should die. But it's up to the emperor to give the final verdict. He decides the *secutor* should die.

The defeated gladiator has been trained not only to fight, but to die well too. He bends down on one knee to await his death calmly. Then the *retiarius* cuts his throat with a quick slash of his dagger.

The amount a gladiator won was agreed beforehand with the organizer of the games. An outstanding gladiator might also be given a laurel wreath.

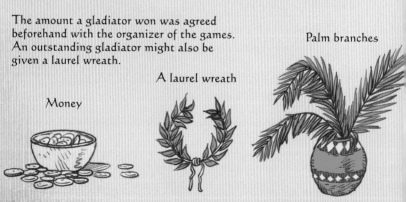

Palm branches

A laurel wreath

Money

* Experts don't know for certain which way audiences turned their thumbs if they thought a gladiator should die.

The emperor rewards the *retiarius* with a branch from a palm tree and a bowl of money. The crowd cheers and the gladiator does a lap around the arena, waving his palm branch.

If the *retiarius* continues as successfully, he might one day be rewarded with the ultimate prize: the *rudis*, or wooden sword, the symbol of freedom.

One-on-one combats between gladiators continue all afternoon. The crowd is loving it. But, just to make sure everyone goes home happy, the emperor orders his servants to throw balls into the audience. Everyone leaps to catch one, knowing they have prizes inside them, that can be collected later.

The prizes were shown as pictures, on vouchers, inside the hollow wooden balls. They probably weren't written out, as most of the poorer citizens couldn't read.

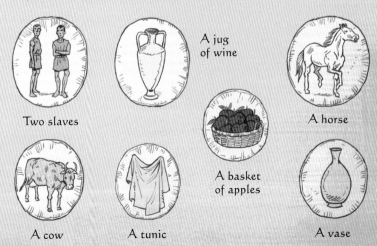

Two slaves

A jug of wine

A horse

A cow

A tunic

A basket of apples

A vase

As time went on, gladiator shows became more and more spectacular. Artificial lakes were built to recreate great sea battles, known as *naumachiae*. Prisoners of war or convicts boarded big battleships, equipped with powerful battering rams to smash and sink the other ships. Thousands often perished in a single contest, either drowned or fatally wounded by the colliding ships.

The *naumachiae* were incredibly expensive: each ship had to move like a real ship in battle, and look like one, right down to the very last detail. All this expense eventually stopped emperors and other officials from including sea battles in their shows. By the second century, they were a thing of the past.

CHAPTER VI

Emperor gladiators

Although they were admired for their bravery in the arena, gladiators were seen as the lowest of the low in Roman society. So it was a shock when some upper class Romans – and even a few bloodthirsty, fame-hungry emperors – took to the arena to fight as gladiators.

The fights between emperors and gladiators were usually fixed, with both sides using wooden swords to make sure there was no risk to the emperor. But according to Roman historians, one emperor, Caligula, didn't play fair.

Caligula kept his face hidden during fights, until he heard jeers from unsuspecting members of the crowd. Then he had them instantly executed. On another occasion, he killed an experienced gladiator by bringing out a real sword in the middle of the fight, and stabbing him to death.

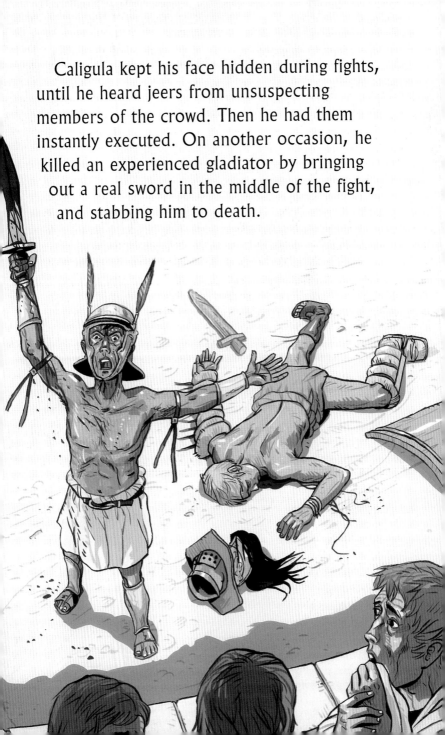

Then, on a powerfully hot day, Caligula removed the canopy that provided shade for the arena and banned anyone from leaving. He wanted to watch the crowd suffer in the heat. His political rivals soon put an end to his reign. He was stabbed to death in the year 41, after less than four years as emperor.

Other emperors, including Nero, Hadrian and Lucius Verus, also appeared as gladiators from time to time.

But there was one emperor who surpassed all others in acts of terror: his name was Commodus and he took part in almost a thousand gladiatorial events. He liked to dress up as the Greek hero Hercules, wearing a lionskin cloak and carrying a club.

Commodus killed hundreds of bears and tigers, though usually from the safety of the royal seats.

Sometimes, Commodus went too far and just looked ridiculous. When he killed an ostrich in the arena, he snatched up its head and thrust it at the Senate as a threat. "We had to chew laurel leaves to keep ourselves from laughing," wrote one of the senators.

But Commodus disgusted people too. He killed gladiators who became too popular and fought against members of the audience who had no protection. He once ordered everyone who had lost their left foot to come

down into the arena. He then flogged them to death with a club and rewarded himself with a million *sesterces* (Roman coins) for his performance – as he did *every* time he fought.

As time went on, Commodus became obsessed with his own importance. After ruling for 12 years, he wanted to reduce the power of the Senate by taking the top office of Consul, too. His mistress Marcia and a senator named Laetus feared for their lives, and decided it was time for him to die. They had Commodus poisoned and then strangled in the bath by the powerful athlete Narcissus.

People had been so horrified by Commodus' vicious acts in the arena that few emperors ever fought as gladiators again.

CHAPTER VII

Fight for freedom

The most famous gladiator of all time was Spartacus, not because of his performance inside the arena, but for his bravery in breaking out of it.

As a young man, Spartacus left his home in the hill country of Thrace, in Greece, to join the Roman army. For reasons we don't know, he ran away, but was captured and sold into slavery. Soon after, he ended up at a gladiator school in Capua, in southern Italy.

Together with another gladiator named Crixus, he planned a dramatic escape. They plotted at night and whenever they could sneak away from the guards.

With his charm and intelligence, Spartacus managed to convince many other gladiators to escape as well.

"Let's make a strike for freedom," he declared, "rather than die for the amusement of others."

At a pre-arranged signal, Spartacus and over 70 other gladiators stole knives, spits and roasting forks from the kitchen and broke out of the school. They also managed to raid carts full of gladiator weapons, before fleeing to nearby Mount Vesuvius. As they ran past wealthy farms and rich men's villas, more slaves flocked to join them.

The Senate was furious when they heard about the rebels.

"You're not to worry," said General Glaber. "Give me 3,000 men and I'll quash them easily."

When the general looked at the map of Mount Vesuvius, he laughed to himself. "The rebels are trapped on the mountain. There's only one narrow path that leads to

the peak and cliffs on either side. I'll slaughter them all."

But Glaber had underestimated Spartacus.

"Slash down wild vines and twist them into ropes," Spartacus ordered his men. "We're going to lower ourselves down the cliffs and surprise Glaber's army from behind."

It was a stroke of genius. Glaber didn't guess what was happening until too late... and the Romans were quickly defeated.

Spartacus spent the winter near Thurii, in southern Italy. News of his success had spread fast and tens of thousands of runaway slaves rushed to join him. More Roman legions were sent to attack them, but each time the rebels were victorious.

The Senate was now taking the revolt very seriously. They sent two enormous armies to finish off the rebels. Spartacus and his men fought them off, but Crixus was killed in the fighting. As revenge for Crixus' death, Spartacus made 300 captured Roman soldiers fight to the death as gladiators.

The rebels then began a long march north, defeating more Roman legions at Picenum, in central Italy, and again at Mutina, in the north.

"We can't defeat the entire Roman army," Spartacus told his men. "Let's escape over the Alps to Gaul."

But his men had other ideas. They wanted to continue looting the countryside and fighting Romans. Spartacus had no choice but to lead them. So they turned south again, with an ambitious Roman general named Crassus in hot pursuit.

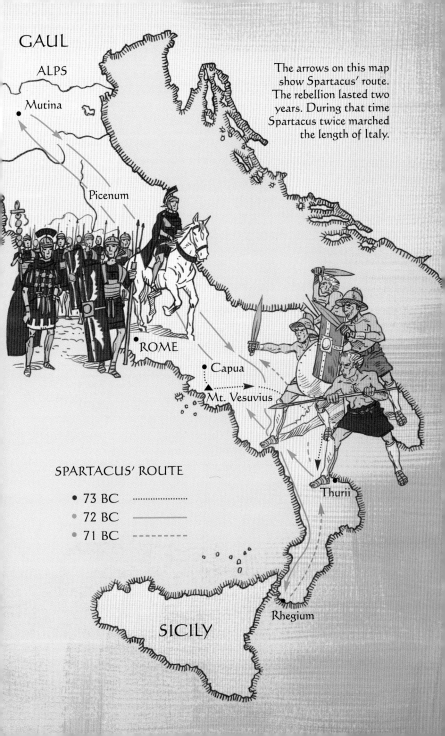

GAUL

ALPS

Mutina

Picenum

The arrows on this map
show Spartacus' route.
The rebellion lasted two
years. During that time
Spartacus twice marched
the length of Italy.

ROME

Capua

Mt. Vesuvius

SPARTACUS' ROUTE

- 73 BC ....
- 72 BC _____
- 71 BC — — — — —

Thurii

Rhegium

SICILY

At Rhegium, on the southern tip of Italy, Spartacus made a pact with a band of pirates. They agreed to let Spartacus and his men board their ships and escape to Sicily, where Spartacus hoped to find support from rebel slaves. But, as soon as they'd been paid, the pirates tricked them and sailed away.

The following year, Spartacus made a push north, but he was soon surrounded by Crassus' army. He made one last heroic effort.

Spartacus gathered up his men and fought a long and bloody battle against Crassus. Spartacus was killed in the battle. Without their leader, the rebel army quickly crumbled. 6,000 were taken prisoner by Crassus and crucified along the Appian way – the road from Capua to Rome – as a warning to other slaves thinking of rebelling.

But the Romans never forgot Spartacus. For two years, he had shown that a Thracian gladiator and a band of slaves could outwit the mighty Roman army.

CHAPTER VIII

How did it all end?

For 800 years, Romans flocked to gladiator shows. In all that time, there is little record of anyone speaking out against all the violence, spilt guts and gore.

Cicero, a brilliant public speaker who lived in the 1st century BC, was one of the earliest critics. He admired gladiators for their courage, but thought the shows were a waste of time and money. He couldn't see how any well-educated man could enjoy the senseless killing of wild animals and the brutal execution of criminals.

A hundred years later came Seneca, a leading playwright and chief minister to the Emperor Nero. He was one of the first to notice the terrible effects of the executions on the crowd. "I come home more greedy, more ambitious, more cruel and more inhuman," he wrote. But nobody took much notice of Seneca, least of all Nero, who thought the games were fantastic.

During the third and fourth centuries, Christian writers began to openly speak out against the games. The bloodthirsty violence went against their religion and culture. They saw the shows as a place that turned men into savages. But even though Christians spoke out against the games, many still went to watch them – often straight from church.

Then came Constantine, the first Christian emperor and the first to try to abolish the games. "We totally forbid the existence of gladiators," he said in the year 325. But it's not clear how serious he was. Three years later, the games were being held as usual and Constantine didn't seem to mind.

Another ban was introduced in the year 404, after a Turkish monk, named Telemachus, came to Rome to protest against gladiator fights. During the performance, he jumped into the arena to try to stop two gladiators from fighting. The spectators were furious. In their anger, they started hurling rocks at him and stoned him to death. Emperor Honorius decided enough was enough and tried to ban gladiators for good.

Not everyone took notice and the shows still continued. But they were becoming less and less popular. Christianity had been the state religion since the year 393, and people's appetite for gladiator shows was dying out.

The Roman Empire was also beginning to crumble, and the games had simply become too expensive to run. The last recorded gladiator fight took place in the year 440. One of the most vicious blood sports ever invented had finally come to an end.

Beast hunts still take place today, in the form of bullfights, in Spain, France, Portugal and Latin America. But all that is left of the gladiator fights are the ruins of the great arenas. No longer spattered with blood, exotic flowers and grasses have taken root in their crumbling stonework. Amazingly, the seeds of these flowers were carried to Rome in the stomachs of wild animals brought from Africa and Asia for gladiator fights all those years ago.

The Colosseum as it is today, illuminated with bright yellow-gold lights. Once a killing ground, where several hundreds of thousands died, it is now one of Rome's most popular tourist destinations.

GLADIATOR GLOSSARY

arena The central area of a stadium, where gladiator fights and wild beast hunts took place.

barbarians The name the Romans gave to people who lived outside the *Empire*.

Consul The most senior government official in the Roman Senate. Two Consuls were elected every year to lead the *Senate* and command the armies.

Emperor The supreme ruler of all Roman lands. Augustus became the first emperor in 27 BC.

Empire (1) All the lands that were controlled by the Romans. (2) The period from 27 BC to the year 476, when Rome was ruled by *emperors*.

Etruscans People who lived in northwest and central Italy, whose civilization flourished between 800 BC and 400 BC.

forum A public meeting space.

gladius A gladiator's sword.

lanista A gladiator trainer, or teacher. The word *lanista* comes from the word *lanius*, meaning butcher.

ludus A gladiator training school.

naumachia A mock sea battle.

Senate The group of men who governed Rome during the *Republic*. The Senate still existed during the *Empire*, but lost most of its power.

Senator A member of the *Senate*.

Republic A country whose rulers are elected by the people. Rome was a republic from 509 BC to 27 BC.

rudis A wooden sword.

GLADIATOR TIMELINE

264 BC   First recorded gladiator game takes place in Rome.

202 BC   Roman general Scipio organizes one of the first big displays of rare animals from North Africa. Audiences are thrilled to see crocodiles, gazelles and elephants.

174 BC   Titus Quinctius Flaminius has 74 gladiator fights at his funeral.

90 BC   Roman general Sulla organizes a fight with Samnite prisoners of war, starting a trend for gladiator fights between prisoners of war.

80 BC   First stone stadium known to us today is constructed in Pompeii.

73 BC   Spartacus breaks out of gladiator school.

55 BC   General Pompey stages an extraordinary beast hunt at Rome's *Circus Maximus*. Twenty elephants are pursued around the arena by untrained hunters. The elephants turn on the hunters, who are all trampled to death. The crowds love it, until the elephants stampede on them. From then on, organizers make sure crowds are better protected during shows.

55 BC   Cicero, a philosopher and politician, speaks out against gladiator shows.

46 BC   The dictator Julius Caesar arranges a sea battle at the Great Games. 3,000 gladiators take part, dressed in Egyptian and Tyrean costume.

Emperor Augustus organizes a sea battle with 6,000 gladiators. This time the gladiators are dresssed up as Persians and Athenians.	2 BC
Emperor Caligula comes to power.	37
Emperor Caligula is stabbed to death by one of his own guards.	41
Emperor Nero bans gladiator games in Pompeii for ten years, after a riot between rival fans.	59
Seneca, a philosopher, playwright and advisor to Emperor Nero, condemns the games.	63-65
Emperor Vespasian begins work on the Colosseum.	70
The Colosseum is opened by Vespasian's son, Emperor Titus.	80
Emperor Commodus is poisoned in the bath.	192
Women gladiators are banned.	200
Emperor Constantine bans criminals from being condemned to train as gladiators (not such a great deal for the criminals – they have to work in the mines instead!)	325
A Turkish monk, Telemachus, is killed trying to stop a gladiator contest.	400
Emperor Honorius abolishes gladiator games.	404

You can find out more about gladiators by going to the
Usborne Quicklinks Website at
www.usborne-quicklinks.com
and typing in the keyword "Gladiators".

At the Usborne Quicklinks Website you will find direct
links to a selection of recommended websites.

Here are a few of the things you can do:

* Explore the Colosseum with an interactive map.

* Dress a gladiator for battle and see if you
pick the right weapons.

* Find out more about the Romans and try some activities.

The recommended websites are regularly reviewed and updated
but, please note, Usborne Publishing is not responsible for the
content of any website other than its own.

Acknowledgements
Photograph: p60 © Reuters/CORBIS

Series editor: Jane Chisholm
Designed by Katarina Dragoslavic
Reading consultant: Alison Kelly, Roehampton University
Additional expert advice from Dr. Mary Beard,
University of Cambridge

First published in 2006 by Usborne Publishing Ltd., Usborne House,
83-85 Saffron Hill, London EC1N 8RT, England. www.usborne.com
Copyright © 2006 Usborne Publishing Ltd. The name Usborne and the
devices ♀⊕are Trade Marks of Usborne Publishing Ltd.